How I Know He's Real

Charlotte E. Woodford
Illustrated by Amanda R. Pretico

Copyright © 2024 Charlotte E. Woodford.

All rights reserved. No part of this book may be used or reproduced by any means, graphic, electronic, or mechanical, including photocopying, recording, taping or by any information storage retrieval system without the written permission of the author except in the case of brief quotations embodied in critical articles and reviews.

WestBow Press books may be ordered through booksellers or by contacting:

WestBow Press
A Division of Thomas Nelson & Zondervan
1663 Liberty Drive
Bloomington, IN 47403
www.westbowpress.com
844-714-3454

Because of the dynamic nature of the Internet, any web addresses or links contained in this book may have changed since publication and may no longer be valid. The views expressed in this work are solely those of the author and do not necessarily reflect the views of the publisher, and the publisher hereby disclaims any responsibility for them.

Any people depicted in stock imagery provided by Getty Images are models, and such images are being used for illustrative purposes only. Certain stock imagery © Getty Images.

Interior Image Credit: Amanda R. Pretico

Scripture quotations taken from The Holy Bible, New International Version® NIV® Copyright © 1973 1978 1984 2011 by Biblica, Inc. TM. Used by permission. All rights reserved worldwide.

ISBN: 979-8-3850-2937-2 (sc)
ISBN: 979-8-3850-2938-9 (hc)
ISBN: 979-8-3850-2939-6 (e)

Library of Congress Control Number: 2024914291

Print information available on the last page.

WestBow Press rev. date: 08/15/2024

To my Mom, thank you for being the first person to tell me that Jesus loves me. To my Mom, Dad, Samuel, and Montana, thank you for never giving up on me. This book is dedicated to all of you.

"For you created my inmost being; you knit me together in my mother's womb," Miss Claire read. Eight-year-old Lilly Greene wasn't a fan of Sunday school, but Miss Claire's teachings brought her delight.

Ever since Lilly was a young child, she has been told that she is fearfully and wonderfully made. "But that is what God says of all children," Lilly muttered.

Mrs. Greene often speaks of a man named Jesus Christ. She says that "He surrendered His life, so that we may live our own."

After encouraging this for a while, that night Lilly's mother finally said to her, "Jesus loves you, Lilly. When you know He's real, accept Him into your heart, and He will change your life forever." This was a difficult matter for Lilly to process, as she often doubted His presence. She prayed that He would somehow reveal Himself to her through His creation.

The next morning, on her walk to the bus stop, Lilly passed her neighbor, Mr. Robbins. "Mr. Robbins..." Lilly said, "How do you know that Jesus is real?" "Well, Lilly," Mr. Robbins remarked, "I know He's real because when I wake up in the morning, the birds sing to me." Lilly acknowledged Mr. Robbins with a smile but was still puzzled.

On the bus ride to school, Lilly pondered over this interaction. "God showed Mr. Robbins that," she thought to herself.

When she saw her friend Henry at school, she couldn't help but ask him the same question.

Henry replied, "I know He's real when I hear my baby sister laugh."

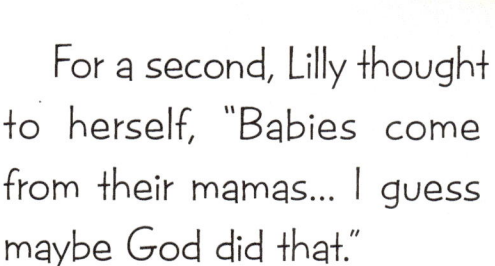

For a second, Lilly thought to herself, "Babies come from their mamas... I guess maybe God did that."

Abigail, sitting right next to the two, said, "Well, Lilly, I know He's real because when it rains, flowers grow."

"My Nana grows flowers in her garden!" Exclaimed Lilly.

Finn joined in and said, "I know He's real because when it snows, each snowflake is completely unique!" Lilly began to remember when they made paper snowflakes in Sunday school, and Miss Claire said the same thing.

Henry, Abigail, and Finn all looked at Lilly and asked, "Lilly, how do you know that Jesus is real?" Unable to respond, Lilly sighed. She didn't have an answer because she was still unsure if He is real or not.

That evening, Lilly, Abigail, and Mrs. Greene walked to the neighborhood creek to watch the sunset. The girls love to explore, and this has always been the perfect way to do so.

As she watched the sunset, Lilly saw an array of bright colors: yellow, orange, pink, and a little bit of purple. All at once, Lilly heard a gentle whisper in her ear, but it wasn't Abigail or Mrs. Greene.

"From the rising of the sun to its setting, my name is to be praised. I created your inmost being, and I knit you together in your mother's womb. I have loved you since before you took your first breath, and I walk alongside you each day. I love you, Lilly Greene; I am real."

Amazed, Lilly didn't have words to speak; she felt a mixture of overwhelming peace and joy.

That night before bed, Lilly said to her mother, "Momma, I know He's real! I know He's real because when I look up, the bright blue sky glimmers down on my face!"

"I know He's real because the birds sing to me in the morning just like they sing to Mr. Robbins!"

"And I know He's real every time you tell me you love me."

"But Momma! Momma! I know He's real because He told me He is when we watched the sunset!" Lilly's mother shed tears of joy as she listened to her daughter speak of her newfound faith.

Finally, Lilly turned to her mother and asked, "After all this time, how do you know He's real momma?"

"Well, Lilly..." her mother said.

"I know He's real because each and every day I see Him in you."

Acknowledgments

To my Lord and Savior, Jesus Christ, it is both a blessing and a miracle to walk alongside you each day. I would not be here if it were not for your unfailing love. Thank you for allowing me, on bended knee, the view of victory in you. I will sing of your love forever.

To my Nana and Papa, Susan and Rick Breckbill, I will never stop thanking you for your continued love and support throughout my life. This book would not have been published if it weren't for you two, and I am proud to be your granddaughter.

To both my Nana and Grandmother, thank you for teaching me how to see the Lord's beauty through His creation. Because of you two, I can look at something as simple as a tree and be reminded of the Lord's goodness.

To my Mom, Dad, brother, sister, and our sweet puppy Sadie, there are not enough words to describe how grateful I am to be a part of this family. I love you guys so much.

To Dr. Timeka Gordon, thank you for believing in me and this book from the beginning. Your knowledge, kindness, and support mean more than I could ever put into words.

To my best friends, Ileana Ferguson, Victoria Velazquez, and Sage Overman, thank you for giving me a newfound perspective on friendship. The three of you have changed my life forever.

Milton Keynes UK
Ingram Content Group UK Ltd.
UKHW052035290824
447531UK00004B/25

9 798385 029389